"I live to make people smile. If I can give you that, then it makes life worth living."

Tommy Leonard

Photo Coutesy of
Bill Higgins • Cape Cod Times

This cookbook is dedicated
to all the children and families
who have already visited Tommy's Place,
and to those that will visit in the future.

It also celebrates the lives of the Angels
who did pass through Tommy's Place doors,
and those who never got a chance.

This cookbook was made with lots of love
for all of you.

Esther Ann Price

Esther Ann Price

TOMMY LEONARD

And folks will wonder what type of man would be so honored. There were those of us who were blessed to have known Tommy Leonard. He was a simple man living an extraordinary life in an extraordinary time. We should all be so simple.

"**Although of meager means**, all of Tommy's undertakings would benefit others. A giver in a world of takers, he was ahead of his time in giving to charity before it became mandatory."

Tim O'Connell and Tommy Leonard met by chance, where else, at a local restaurant. Tim was having dinner and doodling on a napkin, and Tommy was curious about what he was doing. It didn't take long for a bond to form between them, for they shared the same values, beliefs, and principles. The best life came from helping others. Tim's renaming of the Elm Arch Inn to "Tommy's Place" was born out of the desire to give Tommy a "forever home" so he would never again experience being homeless (he was orphaned as a child). Tim also felt that despite their beauty and sentiment, the plaques, memorials, and tributes around Falmouth for Tommy just weren't quite enough to recognize how much Tommy had given and done for others; regionally, nationally and around the entire world. A vacation home for kids with cancer, that could become multiple homes, seemed a much a more fitting way to recognize such a deserving man who dedicated his entire life to helping others.

A compilation from articles by Bob Fitzgerald, Editor/Co-Publisher at New England Runner Magazine and Bill Higgins, Retired Cape Cod Times Sports Editor; along with insights from many discussions with Tim O'Connell.

When the time comes and we have all vanished from this life, there will still be the Tommy Leonard Bridge over Commonwealth Ave.

Tommy Leonard Starting Line Plaque in Woods Hole.

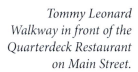

Bench and rock garden overlooking the Atlantic in Falmouth Heights.

Tommy Leonard Walkway in front of the Quarterdeck Restaurant on Main Street.

Tommy Leonard Memorial across the street from the Quarterdeck at the end of the Walkway.

Tommy's Place, a vacation home for kids with cancer named after him.

NOTE FROM TIM O'CONNELL

Tommy's Place is all about families and their entire support system coming together to be there for the family during a horrific time in their lives. Arguably, there isn't anything quite as devastating as a childhood cancer diagnosis. Since the time I first announced the idea of Tommy's Place to the Falmouth community back in 2018, the entire community has welcomed Tommy's Place with open arms from every walk of life.

Businesses large and small have come forward to support Tommy's Place in any way that they can. Individuals have continued to step up in any possible way that they can to support the families that are visiting Tommy's Place. When I was approached with the idea of "you should do a cookbook for Tommy's Place" about two years ago by Esther Ann Price, I immediately said, "no, you should do a cookbook."

The thought that immediately came to mind is that this cookbook shouldn't be by Tommy's Place it should be about the community members coming together to support Tommy's Place. Esther Ann was encouraged to march forward into the community and make this a community-based project and community-based it is! About 50 Falmouth restaurants have come on board to supply a favorite recipe. Businesses have come forward to sponsor the cookbook. Local artist Karen Rinaldo is providing illustrations for the book, New Wave Printing & Design, Inc. is designing and publishing the book and several businesses will be selling the book. A special thanks to Russ Pelletier for coming on board to assist Esther Ann's monumental task of keeping everything organized and to Gail Blakely for editing and being the head taste tester to make sure the recipes are just right. How's that for the Falmouth community coming together!

Tommy's Place Cookbook is all about the entire Falmouth Community "Family" support system coming together to be there for families during a horrific time in their lives - after all, isn't that what Tommy's Place is all about!

Thank you to every single individual and business that has come forward to make this *Tommy's Place Cookbook* possible! We are beyond grateful for the continued help and support of the entire Falmouth community - "Isn't Falmouth Nice" was a one-time community slogan. I think a more appropriate one would be "Isn't Falmouth Amazing!"

Thanks Everyone!!

Tim O'Connell
Tommy's Place, Founder

THANK YOU

TO OUR VOLUNTEERS
WHO TOOK THE RESTAURANT RECIPES,
REDUCED THEM FOR HOME USE,
AND THEN TESTED EVERYTHING!

Roberta Berensen

Maryann Doherty

Paula Driscoll

Michelle Ellis

Donna Jean Jost

Colleen Karsner

Pat Kaufman

Jayne Knapp

Stephanie Mastroianni

Beya Sanquan Oun

Madeline Paquette

Laura Pilcher

Robin Saitz

Alex Satterfield

Carmela Scena

Christine Sullivan

Tom Walrath

Stephanie Walsh

THANK YOU

TO OUR SPONSORS
WITHOUT WHOM PUBLICATION
OF THIS COOKBOOK
WOULD NOT HAVE BEEN POBBIBLE!

BOARD STIFF
193 Main Street
Falmouth, MA 02540
508.540.9555

BOWEN REAL ESTATE OF CAPE COD
162 E. Falmouth Highway
East Falmouth, MA 02536
508.776.2246
John Bowen

CAPE AND ISLANDS DRAPERIES
536 Main Street
Falmouth, MA 02540
508.548.6835
Bill Enos

CAPE COD WINERY
4 Oxbow Road
East Falmouth, MA 02536
508.457.5592
Peter and Erika Orlandella

CLOVER LANDSCAPING
90 Davis Straits
Falmouth, MA 02540
508.540.5539
Gregory McDonald

EXCEL AUTO
94 East Falmouth Highway
East Falmouth, MA 02536
508.444.2777
Pierre Kairouz

FALMOUTH GLASS & MIRROR CO. INC.
537 Teaticket Highway
East Falmouth, MA 02536
508.540.0317
Brian Sundquist

FOR BIRDS ONLY
850 Main Street, Unit 1
Falmouth, MA 02540
508.495.4848
Karen Smith

THANK YOU
SPONSORS

THE GILDED OYSTER
155 Main Street
Falmouth, MA 02540
774.763.5742
Denise, Brian and Meaghan Quinn

HANNOUSH JEWELERS
352 Main Street
Falmouth, MA 02540
508.548.9107
Fadi and Mustapha Akkawi

HOMESPUN GARDEN
174 Main Street
Falmouth, MA 02540
508.475.4441
Beth Chartier-Grier

HOWLINGBIRD STUDIO, INC.
91 Palmer Avenue
Falmouth, MA 02540
508.540.3783
Thomas Clarke

INLET
28 Water Street
Woods Hole, MA 02543
508.388.1848
Beth Colt

INTERGAS, INC.
10 North Main Street
Falmouth, MA 02540
508.548.0704
Joseph Saade

JIMMY'S CLASSIC EATS
22 Luscombe Avenue
Woods Hole, MA 02543
508.540.6823
Beth Colt

JULIO'S UPHOLSTERY
430 Main Street
Falmouth, MA 02540
508.540.1965
Julio Barrows

NORTH FALMOUTH CHEESE SHOP
402 North Falmouth Highway
North Falmouth, MA 02556
508.356.3666
Jennifer Dwyer

OSBORN & RUGH GALLERY
114 Palmer Avenue
Falmouth, MA 02540
508.548.2100
Hillary Osborn and Doug Rugh

THANK YOU
SPONSORS

PATRIOT PARTY BOATS
227 Clinton Avenue
Falmouth, MA 02540
508.548.2626
James Tietje

SHERWIN-WILLIAMS
10 Village Common Drive
East Falmouth, MA 02536
508.548.1770

SIA OPTICAL
311 Main Street
Falmouth, MA 02540
774.763.0366
Christos Canelos

SOFT AS A GRAPE
251 Main Street
Falmouth, MA 02540
508.457.7480

SUPREME PIZZA
147 Teaticket Highway
East Falmouth, MA 02536
508.548.4200

TANORAMA
365 Main Street
Falmouth, MA 02540
508.495.9905
Scott Boyle

TEATICKET MARKET
125 Teaticket Highway
Teaticket, MA 02536
508.540.2713

THE WOODS HOLE INN
28 Water Street
Woods Hole, MA 02543
508.495.0248
Beth Colt

TREEHOUSE LODGE
527 Woods Hole Road
Woods Hole, MA 02543
508.388.4905
Beth Colt

TRENDY TOT CHILDREN'S APPAREL
426 Main Street
Falmouth, MA 02540
508.388.7891
Allison and Nancy Baker

TWIGS OF FALMOUTH
178 Main Street
Falmouth, MA 02540
508.540.0767
Elissa Vancura and Martha Collins

TABLE OF

APPETIZERS 1

    2 **Añejo Signature Guacamole**
       Añejo Mexican Bistro & Tequila Bar

    4 **Baked Brie**
       Grazing Cape Cod

    6 **Brown Butter Miso Cauliflower**
       C Salt

    8 **Pig Candy**
       Quicks Hole Tavern

   10 **Spinach Dip**
       North Falmouth Cheese Shop

SOUPS 13

   14 **Baked Fish Chowder**
       Green Pond Fish Market

   16 **Cheddar Broccoli Soup**
       The Filling Station Food Truck

   18 **Portuguese Kale Soup**
       Dana's Kitchen

   20 **Sea Food Sam's Famous Lobster Bisque**
       Seafood Sam's

SALADS 23

   24 **Brazilian Chicken Salad**
       Bite On The Go

   26 **Natalia's Salad**
       Limani Restaurant

   28 **Nobska Salad**
       The Landfall Restaurant

CONTENTS

BREAKFAST 31

Cinnamon Apple French Toast 32
Persy's Place

Coconut Cornflake French Toast 34
Sacconnesset Golf Club

Loaded Home Fries 36
Devour Artisan Eatery

ENTRÉES 39

Bang Bang Shrimp 40
The Flying Bridge

Cheesy Baked Haddock 42
Falmouth Fish Market

Chicken and Broccoli Pasta 44
Chapoquoit Grill

Chili 46
The Quarterdeck Restaurant

Cod Cakes 48
The Conference Table Falmouth

Cubano Sandwich 50
Quahog Republic

Delicious Baked American Chop Suey 52
Jacks Restaurant and Bar

Epic Crab Cake 54
Epic Oyster

Falmouth Bluefins' Seared Scallops 56
Falmouth Bluefins

TABLE OF CONTENTS
(BECAUSE WE HAVE SO MANY GREAT RECIPES
WE HAD TO ADD PAGES)

ENTREES CONTINUED

58 Farm House Pork Chops
Shipwrecked

60 Fish & Chips
Liam Maguire's Irish Pub

62 Homemade Meatballs
Soprano's Casino By the Sea

64 Lili's Dinnah
Paul's Pizza and Seafood

66 Linguica Mac and Cheese
East End Tap

68 Mussels Possillipo
The Captain Kidd Restaurant and Bar

70 Oyster Rockefeller Casserole
Coonamessett Farm

72 Pastitsio
Estia on Main

74 Sole Rolls
Tommy Leonard

76 Tommy Leonard's Chicken Marsala for Two
La Cucina Sul Mare

78 Vegan Pasta Bake
Bean and Cod

80 The Wally Dog
Wally's Dog Cart

82 West Falmouth Market Chili
West Falmouth Market

SAUCES 85

Escabeche 86
Quicks Hole Taqueria

Fresh Quick Sauce 88
Chef Roland Catering

SIDES 91

Confetti Cheddar Biscuit 92
Coonamessett Inn

Macaroni and Cheese 94
Doggz & Hoggz

Pickle Jar Dill Pickles 96
Pickle Jar Kitchen

SWEETS & TREATS 99

Coffee Angel Pie 100
The Elm Arch Inn

Cookie au Chocolat 102
Maison Villatte

Ice Cream Lasagna 104
Falmouth Senior Center

Mom's Chocolate Birthday Cake 106
Woods Hole Market & Provisions

Power Cookie Recipe 108
Bear In Boots Burger Bar

Rocky Road Fudge Bars 110
The Casual Gourmet

Tiramisu 112
Osteria La Civetta

Vegan Pumpkin Muffins 116
Martha's

APPETIZERS

AÑEJO MEXICAN BISTRO

AÑEJO MEXICAN BISTRO & TEQUILA BAR

188 Main Street
Falmouth, MA 02540
508.388.7631

599 Main Street
Hyannis, MA 02601
774.470.5897

Owner: Jesse Kersey
Executive Chef: Benjamin Phipps

*"Our signature guacamole
has remained a trade secret, until now…*

!Buen provecho!"

Añejo Signature Guacamole

8 to 10 Servings

Ingredients

2 ripe avocados

2 tbsp diced white onions

1 tbsp diced jalapeño

½ tbsp chopped fresh cilantro

2 tsp salt

½ tbsp black pepper

juice of one lime

Directions

Chop the onion, jalapeño, and cilantro. Juice the lime. Set these ingredients aside.

Cut the avocados in half, remove pits, and scoop the pulp out into a bowl. Mash the avocado slightly and begin to add the chopped ingredients.

Be mindful that as avocados vary in size and ripeness you may need more or less of the other ingredients when combining to create a tasty guacamole.

Season with salt and lime juice little by little until the desired flavor is reached.

GRAZING CAPE COD
508.817.2282
grazingcapecod@gmail.com

Owner/Chef: Rachel Rotunno

Baked Brie

6 Servings

Ingredients

1 loaf round country bread, unsliced

1 8-oz round brie cheese

assorted fresh fruit

locally harvested honey *(optional)*

chopped walnuts *(optional)*

Directions

Preheat oven to 400 F.

Cut a circle the size of the brie out of the loaf of bread. Save the extra bread for dipping.

Place the brie in the hole and put bread on a parchment lined baking sheet.

Bake for 15 minutes.

Place bread with brie on a serving plate, surround with fresh fruit. Drizzle some locally harvested Cape Cod honey over brie and top with chopped walnuts.

Serve with crackers and the extra bread, torn into bite-sized pieces.

C SALT

75 Davis Straits
Falmouth, MA 02540
774.763.2954

Owner/Chef: Charles Withers

Brown Butter Miso Cauliflower

2 Servings

Ingredients

1 head of cauliflower

1 white onion

2 cloves garlic

2 tbsp red miso

3 cups heavy cream

½ cup white wine

2 tbsp canola oil

½ cup prunes, pitted

½ cup roasted nuts (walnut / pecan / hazelnut)

8 tbsp butter

3 tbsp aged sherry vinegar

2 tbsp lemon juice

1 bunch fresh mint

kosher salt and freshly ground pepper

Directions

Preheat oven to 350 F.

Slice the white onion thinly. Put the onions into a saucepan with the garlic and canola oil and a sprinkle of salt. Over medium-low heat, sweat the vegetables until translucent, being careful not to add any color to the vegetables.

Deglaze with the white wine and reduce until all liquid is gone in the pan.

Add the red miso and stir. Cook until the vegetables caramelize slightly.

Add heavy cream and bring to a slow boil, then turn the heat down to very low; let simmer for 10 minutes.

Strain liquid out of the pot and pour the vegetables into a blender, with enough liquid to create a thick purée. Taste and season with salt and lemon juice.

Slice cauliflower into 4 equal pieces.

Salt each piece of cauliflower; place in a sauté pan on medium heat with 4 tbsp of butter. Baste the cauliflower "steaks", letting the butter brown around it, until the bottom of the cauliflower is brown and caramelized.

Place the sauté pan in the oven for 5-7 minutes. The cauliflower is done when a sharp knife can be inserted into the middle with no resistance. Remove the cauliflower and place on a rack so that any excess fat drips away.

Cut up the prunes into small pieces, and place in a bowl. Place the remaining butter in a small sauté pan and brown, then pour over the prunes.

Add the sherry vinegar and nuts and stir to combine.

In a serving bowl, make a well in the center of the bowl. Place the roasted cauliflower, brown side up, in the middle of the well. Spoon the prune vinaigrette over the top and sprinkle with torn mint.

Cook's Note:
"Sweating" is a culinary term, often confused with sautéing.
The difference between the two techniques lies in the temperature.
A sauté should be done over medium-high to high heat,
and the goal is to cook quickly while browning the food.

While a sauté can produce a finished meal, a sweat is almost
always a preliminary step in a longer cooking method.

QUICKS HOLE TAVERN

QUICKS HOLE TAVERN
29 Railroad Avenue
Woods Hole, MA 02543
508.495.0048

Owner: Beth Colt
Chef: Sarah (Dufour) Dineen

"Quicks Hole Tavern & Taqueria are huge fans and supporters of Tommy's Place!!

Come in and enjoy our Pig Candy with a cold brew at our bar overlooking the ferry terminal and harbor in Woods Hole or enjoy this recipe at home."

Pig Candy

8 Servings

Ingredients

2 cups brown sugar

2 tsp red pepper flakes

¼ tsp cayenne

1 cup maple syrup

2 tsp ground cinnamon

2 tsp black pepper

¼ tsp salt

2 lbs cured pork belly

Directions

Preheat oven to 350 F.

Cut pork belly into 1" x 3" x ¼" portions. Line sheet tray with tin foil and spray with no-stick cooking spray. Put wire rack on sheet tray and spray wire rack.

Mix all dry ingredients in a mixing bowl; put maple syrup in another mixing bowl.

Dip each piece of pork belly into maple syrup until it's coated. Let excess maple syrup drip off.

Coat pork belly in dry mixture and place on wire rack; make sure to evenly space each piece so they don't stick together when cooking.

Once all pieces are coated, bake for about 20 minutes or until pork belly is bubbling and caramelized.

Remove from oven and allow to cool.

North Falmouth Cheese Shop

NORTH FALMOUTH CHEESE SHOP
402 North Falmouth Highway
North Falmouth, MA 02556
508.356.3666

Owner / Chef: Jennifer Dwyer

Spinach Dip

16 Servings • 1 oz

Ingredients

10 oz box frozen chopped spinach, cooked, cooled, and squeezed dry

16 oz sour cream

1 cup mayonnaise

1 pkg Knorr Vegetable Soup Mix

3 green onions, chopped *(optional)*

Directions

Combine all ingredients and chill about 2 hours.

Serve with cut up raw vegetables *(or other favorite dippers)*.

SOUPS

GREEN POND FISH MARKET

767 East Falmouth Highway
East Falmouth, MA 02536
508.548.2573

Owner: Bob Lewis
Executive Chef: Jim Bentley

Baked Fish Chowder

2 Quarts • 4 Servings

Ingredients

2 large onions, diced

1 cup dry vermouth

6 cups water

1 cup cut up celery leaves, *(trimmed from a bunch of celery)*

2 lbs white fish *(cod, haddock, or hake – no need to cut up as it will fall apart when serving)*

2 cups light cream, warmed

salt and pepper to taste

Directions

Preheat oven to 375 F.

Put onions, dry vermouth, water, and celery leaves in large roasting pan.

Cover with foil and bake for 15 minutes.

Remove from oven and uncover.

Add fish, re-cover pan and bake for 15 more minutes.

Remove from oven, uncover, and add the warmed light cream.

Add salt and pepper to taste before serving.

THE FILLING STATION FOOD TRUCK
Falmouth, MA
401.248.5308
TFSfoodtruck@gmail.com

Owner/Chef: Andrew Swain

Cook's Note:
This makes a very thick soup, but also very delicious.
It's an easy recipe to cut in half—but if you make as it is here,
you will have very happy neighbors.

You might want to thin the finished product while heating,
adding a quarter cup of milk (any percentage) to each serving.

Cheddar Broccoli Soup

8 to 10 servings

Ingredients

2 heads of broccoli, florets cut from stems and set aside

2 cups vegetable stock

1½ cups butter, divided

2 cups milk

1 tbsp fresh chopped basil

1 tsp Sriracha or Tabasco *(hot sauce)*

1½ cups grated sharp Cheddar cheese (6 oz)

1 white onion, cut in coarse dice

1 carrot, cut in coarse dice

1 celery stalk, cut in coarse dice

4 cups heavy cream

1 tbsp salt

½ tbsp black pepper

½ cup flour

½ cup grated Parmesan cheese (2 oz)

Directions

In a soup pot, melt ½ cup butter and sauté the onions, carrots, celery, and broccoli stems.

When tender, add the second ½ cup of butter and the vegetable stock and simmer for 5 minutes. Let cool slightly, make sure all the butter is melted, then carefully purée in a blender or food processor.

Return the purée to the pot and add the cream and seasonings, along with salt and pepper. Bring to a simmer and add the reserved broccoli florets.

In a large soup pot, make a roux to thicken the soup: melt the remaining ½ cup butter over a medium-low heat. Slowly add the flour while constantly whisking. When all the flour is incorporated, lower the heat, and slowly add the milk, continuing to whisk. Once all the milk has been added to the roux, you can increase the heat to medium.

Add the simmering soup broth to the roux, ⅓ of the broth at a time, continuing to stir, and allowing the soup to thicken slightly between each addition.

Finally add the Parmesan and Cheddar and stir well, letting the cheeses melt. Adjust the salt and pepper before serving.

DANA'S KITCHEN

DANA'S KITCHEN
881 Palmer Avenue
Falmouth, MA 02540
508.540.7900

Owners / Chefs: Dana and Arthur Tillman

Cook's Note:
Sweating is a way of softening vegetables over moderate heat, generally in oil or fat, until they become soft, translucent and lose volume due to the evaporation of water during cooking.

Chiffonade is a knife technique used for cutting herbs and leafy vegetables, such as basil or lettuce, into thin strips or ribbons. Stack leaves and rolls into cylinders, then cut with a sharp knife on the bias into slivers.

Make the broth a couple of days in advance. You should always have some homemade chicken broth on hand; it also freezes well, and you can use it in so many ways. Although you can serve it right away, Dana's Kitchen rests the soup in the refrigerator overnight to allow the flavors to marry. Then it is reheated in the morning, used in various dishes, or served for lunch.

Portuguese Kale Soup

40 - 1 Cup Servings (2½ Gallons)

Ingredients

4 tbsp schmaltz (rendered chicken fat) or oil

1½ lbs smoked linguica sausages, sliced into rings

2½ lbs kale, washed, stemmed and cut into chiffonade

2 extra-large Idaho potatoes, peeled, cut into medium dice

1 gallon rich chicken broth, heated *(recipe follows)*

1 large yellow onion, diced

8 cloves garlic, minced

12 oz dried red kidney beans, soaked overnight

salt and pepper to taste

7 to 8 drops hot sauce (Tabasco)

Directions

In soup pot add schmaltz and onions, cover. Sweat onions until soft, 7-8 minutes. Add sausage and heat, covered, 4-5 minutes. Add kale. Season with salt and pepper. Cook uncovered, stirring occasionally until kale cooks down by half and is incorporated into onion-sausage mix about 30 minutes.

Add Rich Chicken Broth, stir well, cover pot and simmer for 1 hour.

Cover beans with cold water, bring to boil. Reduce heat to medium-low and simmer until tender, 25-30 minutes.

Drain and add beans to the soup. Cook potatoes, drain and cool.

Add cool potatoes to soup, bring back to a simmer and add hot sauce.

Rich Chicken Broth

Ingredients

2 whole organic chickens (3 - 4 lbs each) breasts removed for another use

2 lbs yellow onions, chopped

3 sprigs fresh thyme

2 - 5 bay leaves

1 carrot, chopped

1 lb celery, chopped

1 bulb garlic, halved

1 bunch parsley

1 tbsp whole black peppercorns

Directions

Place chickens in stockpot and add water to cover. Bring to boil, skimming and discarding foam as it surfaces.

When stock is boiling, add onions, celery, thyme, bay leaves, carrots, garlic, parsley, and peppercorns. Bring back to boil, lower heat, cover and simmer, 4-6 hours.

Cool the stock and refrigerate overnight. Removed the fat (schmaltz) from top of the broth to use in the kale soup; strain the broth and use.

SEAFOOD SAM'S

356 Palmer Avenue
Falmouth, MA 02540
508.540.7877

Owner / Chef: Michael Lewis

Cook's Note:
Lobster base is sometimes available in fish markets.
A jarred version of lobster base can also be purchased in
most supermarkets, either at the seafood counter
or in the soup section.

This recipe was tested with a 2½ lb. lobster
which provided more than enough meat and "juice."

Sam's Famous Lobster Bisque

4 to 6 Servings • 6 Cups

Ingredients

4 oz butter

1½ cups lobster juice
(save the water after cooking the lobster, this is the "juice")

¼ cup flour

½ to 1oz lobster base

dash of hot sauce

1½ tsp paprika

1¼ cups lobster meat

¼ cup dry sherry

4 cups half and half
(or light cream)

Directions

Add cream to a large pan and place over low heat to begin warming.

In another large pan, place the lobster meat, lobster cooking water, and lobster base. Turn heat to high until it comes to a boil, then reduce to low.

In another large pan add butter, paprika and hot sauce; keep on the lowest setting. When butter is melted, add flour, and stir until smooth and frothy—this is a roux, or thickening sauce. Once it's bubbling, remove it from the stove.

Bring half & half to a complete boil. As soon as it is boiling, add the roux (butter/flour mixture). Whisk well and wait for this to come to another complete boil—then shut off the heat.

Lastly, add the lobster meat and sherry. Mix well, stirring to combine; serve hot.

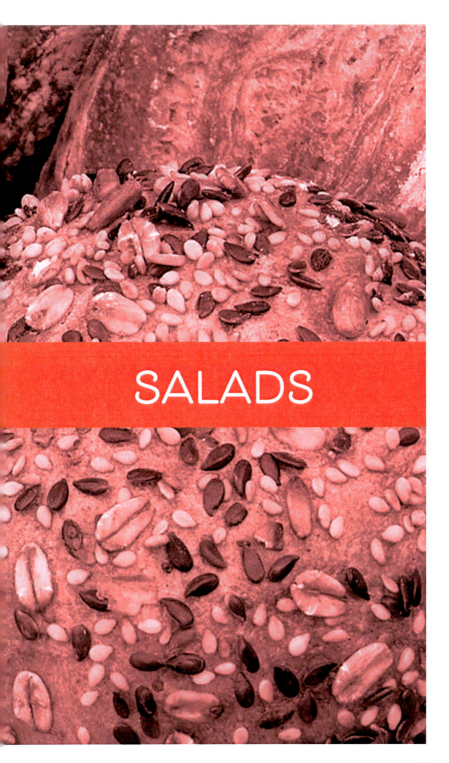

SALADS

BITE ON THE GO
5 Old Meeting House Road
East Falmouth, MA 02536
508.684.8257

Owners: Valerio and Sonia Destefani
Chef: Sonia Destefani

Brazilian Chicken Salad (Salpicão)

8 Servings

Ingredients

2 lbs boneless skinless chicken breasts, poached, cooled and pulled into shreds, not cubed*

1 cup frozen corn kernels, defrosted

1 cup shoestring potatoes (potato sticks)

1 cup frozen peas, defrosted

1 cup shredded carrots

1 cup mayonnaise

½ cup seedless raisins

½ cup sliced stuffed green olives

salt and pepper to taste

Directions

Toss cooked and cooled chicken, vegetables, raisins, and olives in serving bowl.

Add mayonnaise, combine, then gently salt and pepper to taste, remembering that your next step is to fold in the shoestring potatoes, and you don't want it to be too salty—if you are serving later, we recommend that you add the shoestring potatoes right before you serve.

Garnish with green olives and a few shoestring potatoes scattered on top.

*Poached Chicken

Place chicken breast in smallest pot where they fit in a single layer. Cover the chicken with broth or water.

Bring to a boil, then reduce heat to low so liquid is barely at a simmer. Partially cover the pot with a lid and gently simmer for 10 minutes.

Turn off the heat completely and let the chicken remain in the hot liquid for 15 to 20 minutes.

Remove the chicken from the pot; the meat should be cooked through and opaque throughout. Pull into small shreds before using in the recipe.

LIMANI GREEK RESTAURANT
824 Main Street
Falmouth, MA 02540
508.444.6740

Owner / Chef: Natalia Desmersidis

Natalia's Salad

**2 Entrée Servings or
4 Appetizer Servings**

Ingredients

2 lbs cooked beets, peeled

6 scallions

2 cups crumbled Feta cheese

1 tbsp fresh dill

2 tbsp olive oil

juice of half a lemon

salt and pepper to taste

Directions

Set out two large plates or four small plates for entrée or appetizer servings.

Mix the olive oil with 1 tbsp lemon juice in a bowl; set aside.

Slice scallions into ½" pieces.

Slice the beets into ½" pieces.

Finely chop the fresh dill.

Divide the sliced beets among the plates. Top with Feta cheese and sliced scallions.

Drizzle with the olive oil and lemon juice, garnish with dill.

Season to taste with salt and pepper and serve.

Waterfront Dining on Woods Hole Harbor

LANDFALL RESTAURANT
9 Luscombe Avenue
Woods Hole, MA 02543
508.548.1758

Owners: Jim Estes and Katie Stuhlfire
Chefs: Laura Rubino and Mike Deasy

Cook's Note:
Katie suggests using a raspberry vinaigrette dressing and adding grilled chicken to this salad.

Nobska Salad

1 Entrée Serving

Ingredients

2 cups Romaine lettuce

2 oz cut up strawberries

2 oz blueberries

2 oz feta cheese

1 oz candied pecans

Directions

Chop romaine.

Cut up strawberries into quarters.

Arrange romaine on an entrée plate.

Add above ingredients.

Add salad dressing of your choice.

Add a protein if you would like.

Mix all together and serve.

BREAKFAST

PERSY'S PLACE
40 North Main Street
At the Inn on the Square
Falmouth, MA 02540
508.540.3500

Owner / Chef: Joshua Fazio

Cook's Note:
To keep warm while making the topping, place French toast on an oven-safe plate and put in a 250 F oven.

Cinnamon Apple French Toast

4 Servings

Ingredients

French Toast

4 large eggs

1 tsp cinnamon

½ tsp nutmeg

2 tbsp sugar

8 slices toasting bread

Cinnamon Apple Topping

4 tbsp butter

4 green apples, peeled, cored and sliced

2 tsp cornstarch dissolved in ½ cup water

½ cup brown sugar

½ tsp cinnamon

Directions

French Toast

Mix eggs, cinnamon, nutmeg and sugar in a bowl.

Dip bread and fully submerge in the batter.

While bread is soaking, heat skillet to medium on stove; cook on both sides until nicely browned.

Cinnamon Apple Topping

In a large skillet or saucepan, melt butter over medium heat; add apples.

Cook, stirring constantly until apples are almost tender, about 6-8 minutes.

Dissolve cornstarch in water and add to skillet.

Stir in brown sugar and cinnamon; boil for 2 minutes, stirring occasionally.

Remove from heat and serve warm.

Serving

Put two slices of French toast on each plate.

Top with cinnamon apple mixture.

SACCONNESSETT GOLF CLUB

132 Falmouth Woods Road
East Falmouth, MA 02536
508.457.7200

Executive Chef: Drew Grosse
Executive Sous Chef: Alex Satterfield

Cook's Note:
You can also shallow fry in a cast-iron pan or shallow sauté pan:
heat over medium high heat, allowing oil to heat
for about 1 minute.

Coconut Cornflake French Toast

6 Servings • 2 Toasts Each

Ingredients

1 loaf brioche bread

1 14-oz can coconut milk

6 large eggs

2 tsp ground nutmeg

2 tsp ground cinnamon

1 tsp vanilla extract

1 box family size cornflakes crushed into large (Panko) breadcrumb size

vegatable oil

Directions

Cut brioche loaf into twelve ¾" slices and set on a baking tray to dry out, preferably overnight.

Whisk coconut milk, eggs, spices, and vanilla extract.

Crush cornflakes by hand or pulse in a food processor and place them in a large shallow bowl or pan.

Submerge slices of brioche in egg mixture; once the bread is slightly softened, tap off excess and transfer to the cornflake pan.

Shake pan and completely coat bread with cornflakes—flipping and lightly pressing the bread with your hands may help.

Place coated slices onto parchment-lined sheet pans and place in freezer or refrigerator for 15-20 minutes to set.

Preheat a deep fat fryer to 325 F. with about ½" of oil in it.

Carefully place brioche slices into the fryer, dropping the bread away from you; cook for 2 to 3 minutes, until golden brown, then carefully flip with a spatula and cook on the other side until golden brown.

DEVOUR ARTISAN EATERY

352 Main Street
Falmouth, MA 02540
508.540.5900

Owners / Chefs: Aanjes and Hollis Hershfield

"Tommy's Place is a gift to this town and to children and we are honored to be a part of this amazing recipe book showcasing so many wonderful local restaurants."

Cook's Note:
Make it your own by adding crispy chopped bacon, scallions, sour cream, salsa or black beans.
Top it with arugula, spinach or fried egg.

The sky's the limit with this delicious breakfast dish.

Loaded Home Fries

2 Servings

Ingredients

1 lb small red potatoes

2 tsp paprika

½ tsp tumeric

½ cup shredded aged Cheddar cheese

olive oil

Tapatio hot sauce (or another hot sauce of your choosing)

¼ small red onion, thinly sliced

1 tsp garlic powder

1 ripe avocado

nutritional yeast (optional)

salt and pepper to taste

Directions

Preheat oven to 400 F.

Wash and quarter potatoes and slice into ⅛ inch pieces.

Thinly slice one quarter of a red onion.

Place potatoes and onion in a bowl, drizzle with 2 to 3 tbsp olive oil and mix until potatoes are coated.

Add paprika, garlic powder, turmeric to the mixture and sprinkle in some nutritional yeast to taste (1 to 2 tbsp), and a pinch of salt and pepper. Mix again and add more olive oil if needed.

Evenly spread potatoes and onions on a sheet pan; season to taste again with salt and pepper.

Roast in the oven for about 20 minutes or until tender and golden brown.

While potatoes are roasting, shred the Cheddar cheese and dice the avocado into small chunks. Set aside.

Transfer potatoes to a mixing bowl and add Cheddar cheese and toss until the cheese is melted.

Plate potatoes in a serving dish/bowl of your choice. Sprinkle with more nutritional yeast and salt and pepper to taste.

Top evenly with avocado chunks and drizzle the hot sauce over the top, in stripes.

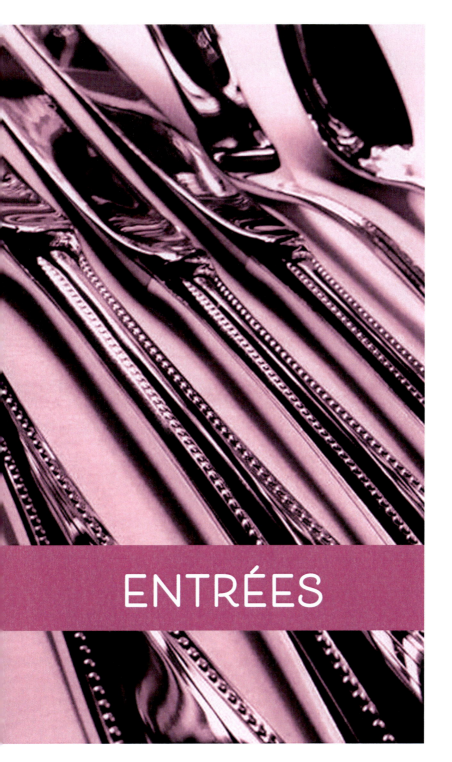

ENTRÉES

THE FLYING BRIDGE
220 Scranton Avenue
Falmouth, MA 02540
508.548.2700

Owner: Linda Zammer
Chef: Stuart Coté

Cook's Note:
*Heavy Mayonnaise is mayonnaise fortified with extra egg yolks, only available through restaurant supply shops. Because it's thicker and slightly richer, has better ability to bind ingredients together, think tuna salad, egg salad or chicken salad. It won't get watery when held in the refrigerator. Regular mayonnaise is fine for home use.

Bang Bang Shrimp

1 Serving

Ingredients

For the Shrimp

8 oz large shrimp, peeled and deveined

1 cup corn starch

1 cup buttermilk

For the Sauce

1 cup Asian sweet chili sauce

1 tsp Sriracha sauce

1 cup heavy mayonnaise*

1 tbsp honey

For the Garnish

salad greens and sliced scallions

Directions

For the Shrimp

Heat canola oil in home fryer to 350 F.

Thaw shrimp if frozen and remove as much water as possible.

Dip the shrimp in buttermilk, shake off excess and dredge in corn starch. Shake off excess cornstarch.

Place shrimp in fryer and cook until batter is crispy, and shrimp are floating. Remove from fryer and place on a plate that is lined with paper towel.

For the Sauce

In a bowl combine Asian sweet chili sauce, mayonnaise, Sriracha sauce and honey. Whisk together until well incorporated.

Mix shrimp in sauce and serve on a bed of greens and top with the sliced scallions.

FALMOUTH FISH MARKET
157 Teaticket Highway
Teaticket, MA 02536
508.540.0045

Owners / Chefs: Edina and David Shahzade

Cheesy Baked Haddock

2 Servings

Ingredients

1 lb haddock (skinned)

½ cup shredded Cheddar cheese

2 to 3 tbsp fresh parsley (chopped)

4 tbsp butter, cut into small pieces

½ to ¾ cup crushed Ritz Crackers

salt and pepper to taste

Directions

Preheat oven to 375 F.

Grease or line a 13 x 9-inch casserole dish with parchment paper.

Lay the fish down in the casserole dish. If there is a tail end, flip the tail under to make the whole piece even in height.

Sprinkle the cheese over the top evenly

Sprinkle the cracker crumbs over the cheese evenly.

Put the pieces of butter all over the top of the crumbs

Sprinkle the parsley evenly all over the top.

Sprinkle a little salt and pepper over the top.

Bake uncovered, 15-18 minutes, until fish flakes easily with a fork.

CHAPOQUOIT GRILL

CHAPOQUOIT GRILL
410 West Falmouth Highway
West Falmouth, MA 02574
508.540.7794

Owner: John Reid
Executive Chef: Clancy Heicher

Chicken & Broccoli with Pasta

2 Servings

Ingredients

2 cups cavatappi pasta

1 cup Cremini mushrooms

12 oz chicken breast

1 cup flour

8 oz crisp white wine (Sauvignon Blanc, Pinot Gris)

3 tsp unsalted butter

fresh herbs of your choice *(suggestions: oregano, parsley, or chives)*

2 cups cut broccoli

2 tsp minced garlic

2 tsp minced shallots

2 cups chicken stock

2 tsp olive oil

salt and freshly ground black pepper

Directions

Preheat oven to 450 F.

Slice Cremini mushrooms, drizzle with olive oil and season with salt and pepper. Place in single layer on a lightly oiled shallow baking pan. Roast for 20 minutes, stirring occasionally.

Cook cavatappi pasta until al dente; drain well.

Lightly steam broccoli and set aside.

Slice chicken breast into ¼ inch strips and dredge in flour; shake off any excess.

Heat 2 tsp olive oil in a large skillet on high heat until oil coats the pan evenly.

Add floured chicken and sauté until golden brown.

Add garlic and shallots and cook for 1 minute.

Deglaze pan with the white wine: lower heat to medium and cook until the alcohol has burned off (about 2 minutes). Add chicken stock, pasta, broccoli, and mushrooms.

Gently simmer for a couple more minutes (adjust heat if necessary).

Add butter, fresh herbs, salt, and pepper to taste; toss together and serve hot.

THE QUARTERDECK RESTAURANT
164 Main Street
Falmouth, MA 02540
508.548.9900

Owner: Bob Jarvis
Chef: Eric Bishoff

After the Eliot Lounge closed in Boston, the Quarterdeck was Tommy Leonard's home base. While working the bar he brought people together. Runners from around the globe would be sure to stop in to see the "guru".

Founder of the Falmouth Road Race and co-founder of the Falmouth Walk, Tommy's legacy continues. The two events bring thousands of people to, as he called it, "Falmouth by The Sea".

Cook's Note:
"Sweat" is a cooking term used to describe a way to soften vegetables. Sweating involves cooking vegetables over a low heat in a small amount of fat in a covered pot (this prevents steam from escaping). The purpose of sweating is to slowly soften vegetable in their own juices so they retain flavor and do not brown).

Chili

4 to 6 Servings

Ingredients

1 lb ground beef

1 lb bell pepper, chopped

1 tsp black pepper

1½ tsp chili powder

2 14-oz cans diced tomatoes

1 14-oz can pinto beans

1 to 2 white onions, chopped

3 cloves garlic, chopped

1½ tsp ground cumin

¾ tsp Worcestshire sauce

2 oz tomato paste

1 chipotle pepper in adobo, pureed

Directions

Brown ground beef in large stock pot.

Cook the beef until no pink remains, stirring constantly to break up the meat.

Remove the beef from the pot and drain all but about 1 tsp of fat; return beef to the pot.

Add onions, pepper, garlic, and spices to pot; sweat until clear vegetables have softened.

Add tomato paste and chipotle pepper; bring to a simmer, then add beans.

Cook for an additional 20 minutes to bring all the flavors together.

THE CONFERENCE TABLE · FALMOUTH

205 Worcester Court
Falmouth, MA 02540
508.540.7136

Owner: Michael Clark
Chef: Colin Fredericks

"Our entire staff was lucky enough to know Tommy in different capacities over his lifetime. His contributions to the Falmouth Road Race have provided countless memories for us and allows us to honor a dear friend by running for the Ryan Richards Foundation.

We are thrilled to provide assistance and help raise awareness for Tommy's Place, as it is a fitting legacy for such a wonderful man."

Cook's Note:
"Sweating" is a culinary term, often confused with sautéing. The difference between the two techniques lies in the temperature. A sauté should be done over medium-high to high heat, and the goal is to cook quickly while browning the food. While a sauté can produce a finished meal, a sweat is almost always a preliminary step in a longer cooking method.

Cod Cakes

4 to 6 Servings

Ingredients

16 oz Cod fish

½ cup white wine

2 stalks celery, small dice

1 tsp minced garlic

2 tsp Dijon mustard

1 tsp smoked paprika

1 tsp fresh thyme

1 sleeve Ritz Crackers, crushed

2 tbsp butter

1 red bell pepper, small dice

1 Spanish onion, small dice

1 tbsp mayonnaise

1 tbsp Old Bay Seasoning

2 tsp fresh lemon zest

½ bunch fresh parsley, chopped

Directions

Preheat oven to 350 F.

Place the butter, wine, and Cod in a baking dish and bake until the fish reaches an internal temperature of 165 degrees. Set aside to cool to room temperature.

In a sauté pan, sweat the vegetables until translucent, and set aside to cool.

Once the cod and vegetables have cooled, combine all ingredients in a large mixing bowl.

Portion the mixture into 6 oz balls, and then press into cakes. In a large pan, on medium heat, sear the cakes until golden brown on both sides.

Serve with a lemon and tartar sauce.

QUAHOG REPUBLIC DIVE BAR
97 Spring Bars Road
Falmouth, MA 02540
508.540.4111

Owners: Erik Bevans and Tom Hughes
Chef: Erik Bevans

Cook's Note:
You can use a small French baguette for this sandwich instead of a sub roll if you prefer.

Cubano Sandwich

1 Serving

Ingredients

1 sub roll

1 tbsp whole grain mustard

1 tbsp butter

1 red onion

¼ cup pickles

2 oz red wine vinegar

3 oz chipotle mayonnaise

2 pieces Swiss cheese

3 to 4 oz Black Forest Ham

4 oz pulled pork

Directions

Preheat oven to 350 F.

Slice red onion "julienne" style: cut slices $\frac{1}{16}$ inch to $\frac{1}{8}$ inch thick, and about 3inches long. Dice pickles.

Cook onion and pickles in red wine vinegar until onions are fully cooked and soft, and set aside.

Mix butter and whole grain mustard together. Coat top of French bread/sub roll with mixture.

Cut Swiss cheese in half.

Cut ham into thin slices . (if necessary)

Build Sandwich

Spread chipotle mayonnaise on inside top and bottom of roll.

Add a slice of Swiss cheese to both top and bottom.

Spread precooked onions and pickles on both top and bottom.

Add pulled pork to bottom half only.

Add sliced ham to top half only.

Place in oven open faced for approximately 8 minutes until all cheese is melted and warmed throughout.

Assemble sandwich with whole grain coated top facing up. Cut diagonally and return to oven to crisp outside of sandwich.

Serve with French fries or coleslaw.

JACKS RESTAURANT AND BAR

327 Gifford Street
Falmouth, MA 02540
508.540.5225

Owners: Jack and Suzanne Sorgi
Chef: Leo Shriner

"We wanted to participate because we know how important it is to us to reach out to the community. Tommy's Place sounds like such a beautiful idea and we at Jacks want to be part of such a wonderful thing."

Delicious Baked American Chop Suey

4 Servings

Ingredients

1 lb ground beef

1 14½-oz can diced tomatoes (or stewed tomatoes)

1 tsp garlic powder (optional)

2 cups shredded Cheddar cheese (or cheese of your choice)

12 oz uncooked rotini or any fun pasta

1 green pepper, chopped

1 medium white onion, chopped

2 tsp Italian seasoning (optional)

3 tbsp canola or olive oil

salt and pepper to taste

Directions

Preheat oven to 350 F.

Boil pasta in a pot stirring occasionally until it is cooked "al dente" (optional - add salt to water). Set aside.

Brown ground beef in large skillet until fully cooked; drain fat and set meat aside.

Place 3 tbsp oil in frying pan; add onions and peppers and cook over medium high heat until softened.

Combine beef, onions, peppers, diced tomatoes, and pasta in a large bowl.

Place all ingredients in a 9 x 13 inch baking dish, sprinkle with salt and pepper to taste, and cover with shredded cheese.

Place in a 350 F oven and cook about 15 to 20 minutes or until cheese is golden brown and nice and melted.

Epic Oyster
shucked to order

EPIC OYSTER
70 County Road
North Falmouth, MA 02556
508.563.3742

Owners / Chefs: Marc and Sarah Warner

Cook's Note:
You can use traditional Tabasco (red) sauce if you cannot find the green.

Epic Crab Cakes
(modified for home cooks)

10 Cakes • 4 oz Each

Ingredients

2 lbs jumbo lump crab meat, roughly broken up

½ cup Ritz Crackers, ground to crumb

1 tbsp Old Bay Seasoning

few dashes GREEN Tabasco Sauce

few dashes Worcestershire Sauce

Panko breadcrumbs, as needed

2 eggs

1 tsp Dijon mustard

1 tbsp finely snipped chives

dash lemon juice

salt and pepper to taste

butter, as needed

Directions

For the Mix

In a mixing bowl, add half of the crab, eggs, Dijon mustard, Tabasco, lemon juice, Old Bay, and Worcestershire Sauce. Fold all ingredients together gently.

Add the Ritz crumbs, remaining jumbo lump crab, and chives to the mixing bowl.

Fold everything together; taste and adjust seasonings with salt and pepper. Chill at least 2 hours, preferably overnight.

For the Cakes

Using a 3 oz scoop, pack mix in flush to top. Form into discs and dredge through Panko crumbs. Layer a half sheet pan with a base of Panko crumbs and place crab cakes on top. Chill the cakes again for an additional 2 hours.

Preheat oven to 350 F.

Heat butter in nonstick skillet and brown both sides of cakes. Transfer cakes to greased sheet pan.

Bake cakes for about 6 to 8 minutes until butter on edges of cakes is sizzling.

Entrées

FALMOUTH BLUEFINS
295 Main Street
Falmouth, MA 02540
774.763.6421

Owner: Andy Baler
Executive Chef: Blake Straubel
Executive Sous Chef: Brock Anderson

"The Bluefin Family all have been affected by cancer in each of our lives and wish to support others through the rough waters of this illness, and to support others in the community and elsewhere."

Cook's Note:
Haricots Verts are slender, French green beans. You can easily roast corn by shucking 1 to 2 ears, cutting off the kernels, and placing them in a small ovenproof skillet. Toss with a little oil and roast in a hot (450F) oven for 6 to 8 minutes, stirring once, until the corn is fragrant and slightly charred.

Falmouth Bluefins Seared Scallops

6 Servings

Ingredients

24 jumbo sea scallops, patted dry

1 cup roasted corn

2 bell peppers (different colors, sliced in strips)

½ shallot, diced

3 tbsp butter

2 oz sauté oil

1 lb fingerling potatoes, cut in half

½ lb Haricot Vert beans

3 pinches fine herbs

salt and pepper to taste

Directions

Heat a sauté pan over medium high heat, then add oil to the pan.

Season the scallops with salt and pepper to taste; when the oil is beginning to smoke add scallops to the pan (carefully without splashing the oil).

Sear the scallops on both sides. You will know when to flip the scallop when the side edged of individual scallop start browning to a dark gold color.

In another pan, over medium high heat, add oil. When it begins to smoke add potato halves flesh side down.

After about 2 minutes flip potatoes and add shallot, corn, peppers, herbs, and Haricots Vert.

Sauté for another 3 minutes until cooked; finish with salt, pepper, and butter.

Serve scallops over the potatoes and green bean mixture.

SHIPWRECKED
FALMOUTH HEIGHTS

SHIPWRECKED

Falmouth Heights
263 Grand Avenue
Falmouth MA, 02540
508.540.9600

Owner: Alex Khan
Chef: Onel Headley

"We proudly serve the Falmouth community and are incredibly honored to be part of such an exciting community project!

We hope this delicious recipe brings joy, full bellies, and happy memories to those who recreate it with their loved ones!"

Farmhouse Pork Chops

4 Servings

Ingredients

1 small onion

2 stalks celery

2 oz butter

1 cup water

½ cup ketchup

2 tbsp Worcestershire Sauce

2 tbsp vinegar

1 tbsp lemon juice

1 tbsp brown sugar

½ tsp salt

½ tsp pepper

8 pork chops, cut ½" thick

2 tbsp cooking oil

1 large green pepper, sliced into rings

1 large onion, sliced into rings

2 sprigs fresh thyme

Directions

Preheat oven to 400 F.

Peel and finely chop small onion and celery.

Combine butter, onion, and celery in a saucepan and sauté until tender.

Add water, ketchup, vinegar, lemon juice, Worcestershire sauce, sugar, thyme, salt, and pepper. Cover and simmer for 20 minutes.

In a skillet, heat the oil and sear pork chops on both sides; place them in a small roasting pan.

Pour the sauce over the chops, top with pepper rings and onion slices. Cover with aluminum foil and place in the oven; bake for 45 minutes.

LIAM MAGUIRE'S IRISH PUB

273 Main Street
Falmouth, MA 02540
508.548.0285

Owner: Deborah Maguire
Chef: Rory Maguire

Liam and Deb opened their pub in August 1994. Within days of opening, Tommy Leonard stopped by to introduce himself and wish the business success. Shortly after opening, Liam and Deb came to know what a legend Tommy Leonard is. They wanted him to pick up a couple of bar shifts, but Tommy remained faithful to the Quarterdeck. He did stop by the pub for a beer or two after work and to watch a baseball game.

"It was always a treat to have Tommy Leonard in the house!"

Cook's Note:
Clam Fry is available at most seafood markets.
If you want to make your own, you can combine 1 cup of corn flour, 1 cup AP flour, 1 tsp salt, 1 tsp freshly ground black pepper, and ½ tsp cayenne pepper.

Fish & Chips

2 Servings

Ingredients

1 lb Cod or Haddock fillet

4 cups Clam Fry Breader Mix

1 tsp Old Bay Seasoning

oil for frying - enough for 4 inch depth in high sided pot (Dutch oven works well)

2 cups beer (we use Liam Maguire's House Pale Ale)

water

deep fry thermometer

Directions

Pour oil into a deep sided pot. And heat to 375 F.

Set up a prep work area for dipping fish in dry Clam Fry mix, water, and batter.

Cut fish fillets into 4 to 6 inch pieces and pat dry.

Mix 2 cups Clam Fry Breader Mix and beer together. (The batter should be "pourable" in thickness.) Add Old Bay Seasoning to batter.

When oil has reached correct temperature, dip filet in dry Clam Fry Breader Mix, water, then back in dry mix.

Then using tongs, dip coated fish fillet into Clam Fry batter and place in hot oil.

Cook the fish until batter is golden brown, and filet is floating at the top of the oil. Remove from oil and place on paper towel lined plate.

Repeat with remaining filets, making sure cooking oil maintains at 375 F.

Serve with fries, cole slaw and a wedge of lemon.

SOPRANO'S CASINO BY THE SEA

286 Grand Avenue
Falmouth, MA 02540
508.548.7800

Owner: John Richardi
Chef: Michael DePaolo

Homemade Meatballs

25 4-oz Meatballs

Ingredients

5 lbs ground beef

¼ cup minced garlic

¼ cup minced shallots

1½ tbsp salt

1½ tbsp pepper

1 cup grated Parmesan cheese

1½ tbsp dried basil

¼ cup chopped parsley

5 large eggs

2 cups Italian breadcrumbs

Directions

Preheat oven to 350 F.

In a large bowl mix ground beef, garlic, shallots, eggs, and Parmesan cheese until fully blended.

Add salt, pepper, dried basil, and breadcrumbs to the bowl.

Mix all ingredients thoroughly and roll into balls.

Place on baking sheet lined with parchment paper.

Cook at 350 F for 25 minutes in the oven.

PAUL'S PIZZA AND SEAFOOD
14 Benham Road
Falmouth, MA 02540
508.548.5838

Owner: Peter Muse
Chef: Liliane Stone

Cook's Note:
Chourico is a Portuguese sausage easily available in supermarkets on Cape Cod. You can use linguica or kielbasa if you cannot locate chourico.

For this recipe, remove the casing from the sausage and crumble the meat inside; alternately, you can rough chop the sausage meat and use it that way.

Lili's Dinnah

1 Serving

Ingredients

1 lb mussels

2 oz chopped plum tomato

1 tsp salt

1 tsp garlic

2 oz chicken stock

4 oz cooked, thin spaghetti

2 tbsp chopped leeks or scallions

2 oz crumbled chourico sausage

1 tsp pepper

2 oz white wine

1 tbsp butter

shaved Parmesan cheese (optional)

Directions

Heat a pot of water and leave on stove top on medium.

In a saucepan, place all the ingredients except spaghetti and mussels and turn heat to high.

When butter has melted add mussels and cover the pan. After one minute, toss or stir ingredients. Continue tossing or stirring periodically until all mussels have opened.

Reheat spaghetti by dipping into hot water and draining.

Place spaghetti into a large bowl and pour mussels and sauce over the top.

Garnish with shaved Parmesan, if desired, and serve with a side of crusty garlic bread.

EAST END TAP
734 Teaticket Highway
East Falmouth, MA 02536
508.444.8677

Owners / Chefs: Paul and Ellen Pendleton

"We chose to share the Linguica Mac and Cheese because kids love it. Although we offer a "Kids Mac & Cheese', they favor the Linguica Mac". It's so yummy kids have requested it sent airmail!!

But that's a story for another day."

Cook's Note:
Linguica is readily available in most supermarkets on Cape Cod. You can use any other pre-cooked spicy sausage such as kielbasa if you wish.

Linguica Mac and Cheese

PAN FRIED LINGUICA SAUSAGE AND ROASTED RED PEPPERS IN A CREAMY WHITE CHEESE SAUCE TOSSED WITH MARCONI, TOPPED WITH TOASTED BREADCRUMBS

1 Serving

Ingredients

6 oz elbow macaroni

½ cup Portuguese linguica sausage, roughly chopped

¼ cup roasted red peppers, roughly chopped

¾ cup heavy cream

1¼ cup shredded white Cheddar cheese

2 tbsp toasted Panko breadcrumbs (pre-mixed with butter and paprika)

Directions

In boiling water cook macaroni to al dente (slightly undercooked). Drain and set aside.

In a sauté pan, over medium heat, sauté linguica and peppers for 1 to 2 minutes to release oils.

Add heavy cream and bring to boil on high heat; allow to simmer for 1 to 2 minutes to reduce the sauce.

Add white Cheddar, simmer over medium heat until it is melted.

Add pre-cooked macaroni, toss, pour in bowl, top with breadcrumbs and serve.

THE CAPTAIN KIDD RESTAURANT AND BAR

77 Water Street
Woods Hole, MA 02543
508.548.8563

Owner: William "Blackie" Murray
Chef: Frank Belfiore

Cook's Note:
"Serve the mussels with their sauce in a big bowl or over pasta. Or, meander down to the Captain Kidd and enjoy the dish along with a great view of Eel Pond."

Mussels Possillipo

2 Servings

Ingredients

1 tbsp olive oil

1 green pepper, sliced

1 onion, sliced

4 lbs mussels, scrubbed and de-bearded

1 tsp each: basil, thyme, oregano, parsley flakes and crushed red pepper flakes

½ lb mushrooms, sliced

1 14½-oz can diced tomatoes

2 cups white wine

Directions

Heat olive oil. Sauté garlic, peppers, onion, and mushrooms for 4 minutes.

Add oregano, thyme, basil, parsley, red pepper flakes, tomatoes, and wine. Bring to boil; let simmer for 5 minutes.

Add mussels, cover, and cook over high heat until the mussels have opened, about 5 minutes.

Coonamessett Farm

COONAMESSETT FARM

277 Hatchville Road
East Falmouth, Massachusetts 02536
508.563.2560

Owners / Chefs: Ron and Roxanna Smolowitz

Cook's Note:
An easy way to shuck oysters for a dish like this is to roast them in a super-hot oven just until the top shell pops about ¼ inch open from the bottom. Then pull the top shell of each bivalve off by hand, with a little help from a butter knife for leverage. The recipe needs a single layer of oysters to cover with the topping so be sure to choose the appropriately sized casserole dish.

Oysters Rockefeller Casserole

4 to 8 Servings

Ingredients

1 qt fresh oysters, shucked

1 cup chopped onion

3 cups chopped greens or drained frozen spinach

1 cup white sauce*

hot sauce to taste

3 tbsp butter

½ cup chopped celery

1 cup breadcrumbs

½ cup Parmesan cheese

Worcestershire sauce, to taste

*White Sauce

2 tbsp butter

¼ tsp salt

few dashes nutmeg

2 tbsp flour

⅛ tsp black pepper

1 cup milk

Directions

Heat oven to 450 F.

Butter bottom and sides of casserole, place oysters in a single layer and set aside.

Sauté onion and celery in butter, when soft add greens or drained spinach and continue to cook.

Add cup of white sauce or a can of creamed mushroom soup to the mix as if you were making creamed spinach. Add breadcrumbs and Parmesan cheese. Season with Worcestershire and hot sauce to taste. Pour this mixture on top of oysters.

Bake for 30 minutes. Remove and cover with grated Cheddar cheese and breadcrumbs.

Place back in oven until brown; about 10 minutes.

*White Sauce

Melt butter in a sauce pan over low heat; whisk in flour, add ¼ tsp salt, ⅛ tsp black pepper and a few dashes of nutmeg.

Gradually whisk in milk, heat to boiling, stirring constantly for 1 minute.

Cook over medium heat until smooth and bubbly, whisking occasionally.

ESTIA ON MAIN
117 Main Street
Falmouth, MA 02540
508.548.3300

Owners: The Markantonis Family
Chef: Emerson Pinto

Cook's Note:
This classic casserole can also be prepared with ground lamb if you prefer.

Pastitsio

6 to 8 Servings

Ingredients

1 lb ziti
(or other short tubular pasta)

2 tbsp extra virgin olive oil

2½ lbs ground beef

1 medium onion, diced

1 cup tomato paste

3 tbsp dried oregano

1 tbsp dried parsley

½ tbsp minced garlic

1 tsp salt

½ tsp black pepper

For Binder

3 whole eggs

1 cup heavy whipping cream

¾ cup grated Pecorino Romano cheese, divided

For Béchamel

6 tbsp flour

6 tbsp butter

1 quart whole milk

½ tbsp lemon juice

1 tsp salt

½ tsp pepper

1 tsp Cajun seasoning

Directions

In a large saucepan, sweat onion in 1 tbsp olive oil on low heat.

Add ground beef to onion and sauté until brown, then drain off the fat.

Add tomato paste, black pepper, oregano, garlic, parsley, and salt, and stir to combine.

In a separate pot, cook pasta until al dente; drain, rinse, and place in a large mixing bowl.

Add 1 tbsp oil to the pasta and stir to combine.

Prepare binder: mix eggs with ½ cup cheese and cream; stir into the pasta.

Prepare Béchamel: melt butter in a medium saucepan, slowly add flour, whisk in milk and bring to simmer until thickened.

Add salt, Cajun spice and lemon juice and mix well.

In a 9" x 13" baking pan, assemble the Pastitsio in layers: pasta, meat sauce, and Béchamel.

Top with remaining ¼ cup Pecorino Romano cheese.

Bake at 350 F for approximately 35 minutes or until top is slightly golden: let rest 15 minutes before serving.

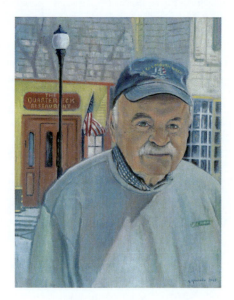

TOMMY LEONARD

"In 1993, The Falmouth Road Race printed a cookbook with recipes from many World Class Runners, the mayor of Boston Ray Flynn and one from Tommy Leonard.

When I first read thru that booklet, I was shocked to find a recipe from my friend Tommy. I know firsthand that Tommy had trouble making toast but was very good at setting off the smoke alarm.

So, was this really his recipe?
We'll never know, but I thought it would be a nice entry."

Russ Pelletier

Sole Rolls

4 Servings

Ingredients

1 lb filet of sole (about 4 pieces)

⅓ lb scallops, chopped

2 oz fresh baby bella mushrooms, sliced

3 tbsp butter, divided

1 sleeve Ritz Crackers, crushed (set aside some for topping)

¼ cup white wine *or a whole bottle—he probably drank most of it!*

Directions

Preheat oven to 350 F.

In a mixing bowl, combine Ritz Crackers, sliced mushrooms, and scallops, 2 tbsp melted butter and ¼ cup white wine.

Lay the filets out and place the stuffing mixture at one end of each piece of sole.

Roll the filets up starting at the end with the stuffing. Secure the roll using a toothpick and put in a baking dish (an 8" x 8" pan works well). Place any extra stuffing into the dish along the sides.

Melt remaining tbsp butter and stir in 2 tbsp wine: brush over rolls, dust with remaining cracker crumbs.

Bake about 20 minutes, until the fish flakes easily and the breadcrumbs start to brown.

LA CUCINA SUL MAR
237 Main Street
Falmouth, MA 02540
508.548.5600

Owners: Mark and Cynthia Cilfone
Chef: Mark Cilfone

"Tommy used to love to come in and take a seat at the bar and chat with the staff and the patrons. It always helped him work up an appetite to enjoy one of his favorite meals, the Chicken Marsala."

Cook's Note:
Veal Demi-Glacé may be difficult to find, but you can substitute jarred chicken bouillon if you need to. AP flour is unbleached, all-purpose flour.

Tommy Leonard's Chicken Marsala for Two

2 Servings

Ingredients

4 4-oz chicken breasts, boned
2 tbsp olive oil
2 tbsp butter
3½ tbsp veal demi glacé
2 cups sliced mushrooms

1 cup AP flour
1 tbsp chopped shallots
2 cups Marsala Wine
1 tsp sugar
salt and pepper to taste

Directions

Place the chicken breasts between two pieces of plastic wrap. Using a meat mallet or a small frying pan, pound the chicken until there is an equal thickness throughout the breast, being careful not to over pound or tear the chicken.

Flour each breast, shaking off excess flour.

Put two tbsp of olive oil in a large sauté pan. Place over medium high heat and heat the olive oil—do not overheat to the point where it smokes but have it hot enough so the chicken sizzles when placed in the pan.

Place the chicken carefully in the sauté pan. Brown the chicken on both sides, then add the chopped shallots, sliced mushrooms, and butter. Cook until shallots are just barely browned. Remove pan from heat and add the Marsala wine.

Place the pan back on the burner and ignite the Marsala. Wait until the alcohol burns off, then add the veal demi-glacé and sugar; reduce to medium.

Cover the pan and let the chicken breast finish cooking. It should take about one and a half to two minutes. Don't be afraid to check the chicken—add a little water if the sauce is too thick.

Tommy used to like this with angel hair pasta and a crusty piece of bread.

BEAN AND COD
145 Main Street
Falmouth, MA 02540
508.548.8840

Owners / Chefs: Sharron and Steve Vannerson

"We first met Tommy Leonard in the mid-1990's when he was a bartender at the Eliot Lounge in Boston, and we managed a Steve's Ice Cream next door on Mass Ave.

Fast forward a dozen years to Falmouth and Tommy is asking us at Bean and Cod to make cookies to support his charity walk during Road Race Weekend.

We could not have been happier to support his cause."

Cook's Note:
"This recipe uses silken tofu in place of a dairy product to create a creamy tomato sauce base for a baked pasta dish. We use brown rice penne and gluten-free breadcrumbs (optional), creating a gluten free and vegan entrée, a combination that is sometimes hard to find. But don't tell your family. They won't know it as anything other than a comfort food casserole with pasta and veggies."

Vegan Pasta Bake

4 to 6 Servings

Ingredients

1 small eggplant, ½" dice

1 small zucchini, ½" dice*

½ lb Cremini or Baby Bella mushrooms, quartered

½ cup onion, ½" dice

¼ lb kale*

1 package silken tofu

¾ tsp salt

½ tsp pepper

¾ tsp garlic powder

1 tsp oregano

2 cups marinara sauce**

1 cup brown rice pasta***

as needed, extra virgin olive oil (EVOO)

Directions

Preheat oven to 350 F.

Roast veggies with a sprinkle of EVOO and a pinch of salt. Zucchini for 5 minutes, eggplant 7 minutes, mushrooms 10 minutes.

Sauté onions in EVOO.

Blanch kale with a pinch of salt. Squeeze dry and chop.

Mix tofu in blender or Cuisinart with the seasoning; salt, pepper, garlic powder and oregano. Stir together with marinara, then fold in veggies.

Boil pasta 7 minutes, stirring frequently to prevent the pasta from sticking together, drain and add to sauce mix.

Turn into greased (use canola spray) 8 x 8-inch pan. If doubling, a deep 9 x 13-inch will work.

Bake 30 to 35 minutes.

---

* Use either kale or zucchini or both to add some green to the dish.
** Any sugarless brand, like Bobo's.
*** Tinkyada brand penne, cooked in only 7 minutes, not the 12 minutes on the package.

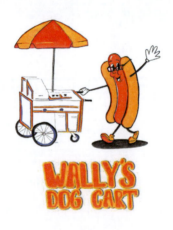

WALLY'S DOG CART
Falmouth, MA
708.655.6314

Owners / Chefs: Tom & Kathy Walrath

"Participating in this project is easy for me.
I had known about Tommy Leonard most of my adult life,
as I stayed in Falmouth with family and bought a home here in 2000.
I got to know him through the Falmouth Walk, as a Co-founder
of this great cause. Tommy shared his memories of Chicago
with me, and we talked baseball, especially since he was a
Cardinals fan and I rooted for the Cubs!

I'm a better man for having met Tommy Leonard!
Helping to support Tommy's Place has been easy for me.
From the first time I met Tim O'Connell and he shared
his idea of creating Tommy's Place,
I knew this is something that I wanted to help with."

The Wally Dog

1 Serving

Ingredients

1 Vienna beef frank

1 poppy seed bun

Optional Toppings

Vienna yellow mustard

freshly chopped onion

Vienna Kosher dill pickle spear

Dash of Vienna celery salt

Vienna Chicago style green relish

2 tomato wedges

2 Vienna sports peppers

Directions

Heat in water, steam, or grill the genuine article—a Vienna beef frank.

Nestle the frank in a steamed poppy seed bun.

Then pile on the toppings in the order listed.

WEST FALMOUTH MARKET

623 West Falmouth Highway
Falmouth, MA 02540
508.548.1139

Owners / Chefs: Danielle and Tom Johnson

West Falmouth Market is an old-fashioned country store, with a butcher shop, deli and bakery that has been a staple of the community since 1902.

The current owners chased their dreams and purchased the market in 2016 after Tom's personal battle with cancer.

WFM Chili

16 Servings

Ingredients

2 yellow onions

1½ lbs pulled pork

3 oz pureed chipotle in adobo

3 cups diced tomatoes

1 cup chili powder

½ cup cumin

1 tbsp black pepper

12 cups cooked black beans

2 bell peppers

1½ lbs smoked brisket

6 cups chili sauce

2 cans Guinness Beer

½ cup paprika

¼ cup garlic

2 tbsp vegetable oil

½ lb semi-sweet chocolate chips

Directions

Dice all vegetables then sauté over medium high heat in 2 tbsp of vegetable oil for 3 minutes.

Add all seasonings along with salt to taste and continue cooking for 1 minute.

Add chipotle and mix.

Empty beer into the pot and bring to a boil.

Add all remaining ingredients except for chocolate chips and bring to a simmer.

Turn heat down to low, add the chocolate chips over the top and cook for 30 minutes.

SAUCES

QUICKS HOLE TAQUERIA

6 Luscombe Avenue
Woods Hole, MA 02543
508.495.0792

Owner: Beth Colt
Chef: Nat Summerton

Escabeche
GREAT ON TACOS!

8 Servings

Ingredients

½ cup granulated sugar

2 tbsp kosher salt

1 jalapeño, sliced into thin rings, seeds intact

2 small red onions, julienned

½ cup canola oil or canola/olive oil blend

1½ cups red wine vinegar

2 large carrots, peeled and thinly sliced on bias

½ cup minced garlic

½ tbsp coarse ground black pepper

Directions

Bring vinegar to a boil in a sauce pot; add in sugar and kosher salt and stir until dissolved. Remove from heat and chill mixture.

Cut up carrots, jalapeño, garlic, and red onion; combine with oil and pepper in place in an airtight container.

Once vinegar mixture has cooled to at least room temperature, pour over vegetable mixture, seal, and shake gently to mix. Make sure vegetables are covered.

Refrigerate at least two hours, or overnight for best flavor.

Store refrigerated up to one week.

CHEF ROLANDS CATERING

CHEF ROLANDS CATERING

800 Falmouth Road
Mashpee, MA 02649
508.539.0001

Owner: Matt Lombardo
Chefs: Roland and Patricia Lamirande

Cook's Note:
Perfect for fish, chicken, scallops, and shrimp.

Fresh Quick Sauce

6 to 8 Servings

Ingredients

6 large ripe tomatoes, cut into ¾" dice

5 cloves garlic, minced

4 tbsp tomato paste

2 tbsp cane sugar

½ cup olive oil

1 large sweet onion, cut into ¼" dice

2 fennel bulbs, lightly steamed and cut into ¾" dice

⅓ cup fresh basil puree

½ cup grated Pecorino Romano cheese

salt and pepper to taste

Directions

Preheat oven to 375 F.

Toss steamed fennel with ⅓ of the olive oil. Roast in the oven for 18 to 20 minutes.

In heavy Dutch oven, sauté onions and garlic in remaining olive oil.

Add tomatoes and cook over low heat for 20 minutes.

Fold in roasted fennel and tomato paste.

Cook for 10 more minutes.

Finish with basil puree, grated cheese, and sugar.

Add salt and pepper to taste.

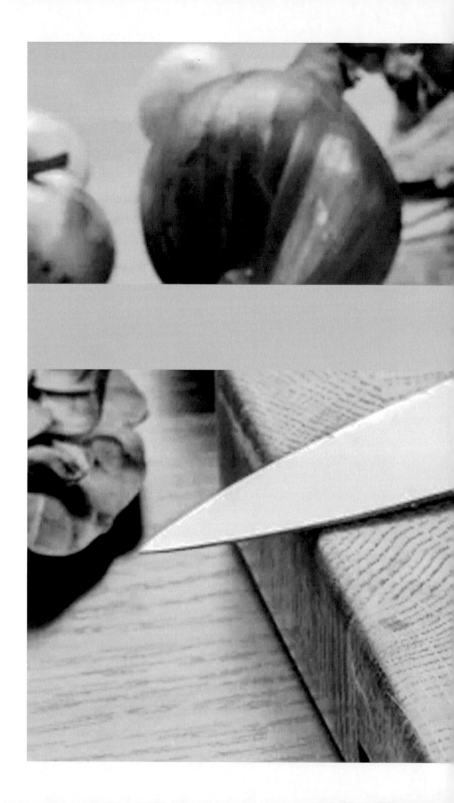

SIDES

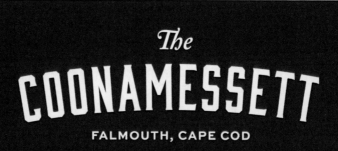

THE COONAMESSETT INN RESTAURANT

311 Gifford Street
Falmouth, MA 02540
508.548.2300

Owner: Lark Hotels
Chef: Ricky Smith

Cook's Note:
AP flour is all-purpose flour - unbleached is preferable.

Confetti Cheddar Bisquit

16 Large Bisquits

Ingredients

6 cups AP flour

1 tbsp fresh ground black pepper

1½ tsp garlic powder

¾ tsp cayenne pepper

3 cups buttermilk

¼ cup each, small diced - green, yellow and red bell peppers

2 tbsp baking powder

2 tbsp sugar

1½ tsp baking soda

3 cups shredded sharp Cheddar cheese

¾ cup mayonnaise

melted butter, for brushing on tops

flaky sea salt and black pepper to finish

Directions

Preheat oven to 375 F.

Grease baking sheet with cooking spray.

Whisk together dry ingredients in a large bowl, add cheese and toss to coat. Make a well in the center.

Whisk together the buttermilk and mayonnaise in a separate bowl.

Pour the buttermilk and mayonnaise mixture into the well and stir until incorporated.

Fold in the peppers, taking care not to work the dough too much.

Shape to desired size (about ⅓ cup each) then place dough one inch apart on the baking sheet.

Brush the tops with melted butter and sprinkle with the flaky sea salt and pepper.

Bake 15 to 20 minutes, until golden brown. (If internal temperature is 200 F, they are done - remove from baking sheet and cool on a wire rack.)

Store in airtight container when cool.

SIDES

DOGGZ & HOGGZ

781 Main Street
Falmouth, MA 02540
508.548.3663

Owners / Chefs: Mike and Linda Bullard

"I grew up in Falmouth, left for a while to live in Florida and eventually came back. Along with my wife Linda, I wanted to bring new foods and flavors to my hometown.

We are part of this cookbook because Tommy's Place is part of this town—and we are part of this town."

Macaroni and Cheese

6 to 8 Servings

Ingredients

8 cups water

2 cups pasta

1 cup cream

½ cup Swiss cheese, shredded

½ cup smoked Gouda, shredded

½ cup Cheddar cheese, shredded

1 tsp chicken bouillon base

1 to 2 tsp tumeric

1 tsp vegetable oil

salt and pepper to taste

chopped chives (optional)

Directions

Add oil, a dash of salt and pepper, and chicken base to the 8 cups water and bring to a boil.

Add pasta and cook until done. DO NOT DRAIN PASTA.

Mix in cream, then add turmeric and cheeses; let cheeses melt.

Pour into a baking dish or pan and let cool for about an hour so mixture can thicken.

Add chives, if desired, for garnish.

PICKLE JAR

THE PICKLE JAR KITCHEN
170 Main Street
Falmouth, MA 02540
508.540.6760

Owners: Benjamin Gallant, Casey Gallant, Lis Lay
Chef: Benjamin Gallant

"We became friendly with Pete and Pam Richardson, the previous owners of the Elm Arch Inn. Our kids would play soccer together.

Tommy used to stop by the Pickle Jar for breakfast in his later years. He was a kind man.

We are excited that Tommy's Place became a reality in such a historic spot, named after a great man, for a wonderful cause!"

Pickle Jar Kitchen Dill Pickles

10 to 12 Servings
(unless you love pickles - then 1 serving)

Ingredients

4 cups water

1 tbsp sugar

4 to 6 pickling cucumbers, cut into spears

1 handful fresh dill, whole

1 tsp dill seed

½ tsp whole black peppercorns

1 jalapeño (optional), cut in half, with or without the seeds

1¼ cups white vinegar

1 tbsp sea salt or kosher salt

2 to 4 cloves garlic, whole and peeled

½ tsp whole coriander

½ tsp whole yellow mustard seed

½ tsp juniper berries

Directions

Place pickle spears, garlic, fresh dill, and jalapeño (optional) in a large container, jar, or bowl with enough room to cover cucumbers with liquid.

Bring water, vinegar, salt, sugar, and spices to a boil. Cool slightly, but while still very warm, pour over cucumbers.

Let cool completely, making sure that the cucumbers are covered with liquid. (They may float a bit.)

Cover tightly and refrigerate for 2 to 3 days before enjoying. You can eat them sooner if you want. They last a few weeks in the fridge.

SWEETS & TREATS

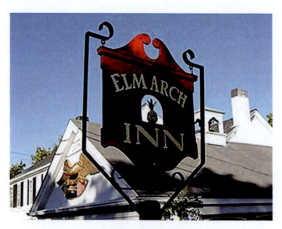

THE ELM ARCH INN
26 Elm Arch Way
Falmouth, MA 02540

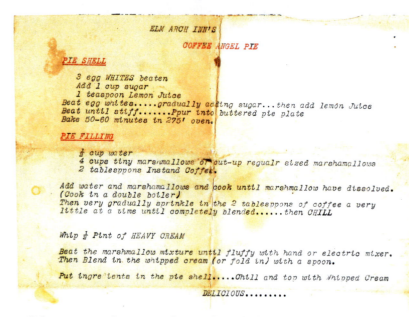

"This is a copy of an original recipe from the kitchen of The Elm Arch Inn.

It dates back to the 1930's, possibly 1933.

Graciously provided to us by Peter and Pam Richardson,
the third generation of the Richardson Family to run the Inn,
and the last in the longest line of innkeepers in our community."

Elm Arch Inn's Coffee Angel Pie

1 Pie

Ingredients

Pie Shell

3 egg WHITES, beaten

add 1 cup sugar

1 tsp lemon juice

Pie Filling

½ cup water

4 cups tiny marshmallows or cut up regular sized marshmallows

2 tbsp instant coffee

Topping

½ pint heavy cream

Directions

Pie Shell

Beat egg whites ... gradually adding sugar ... then add lemon juice. Beat until stiff.

Pour into buttered pie plate.

Bake 50 to 60 minutes in 275 F oven.

Pie Filling

Add water and marshmallows and cook until marshmallows have dissolved. (Cook in double boiler.)

Then very gradually, sprinkle in the 2 tbsp of coffee a very little at a time, until completely blended ... then chill.

Whip 1/2 pint of heavy cream.

Beat the marshmallow mixture until fluffy with hand or electric mixer. The blend in the whipped cream (or fold in) with a spoon.

Put ingredients in the pie shell ... chill and top with whipped cream.

DELICIOUS ....

MAISON VILLATTE

267 Main Street
Falmouth, MA 02540
774.255.1855

Owner / Chef: Boris Villatte

"Owner Boris Villatte was one of the men behind the PB Boulangerie in Wellfleet and once headed up the bakery at Las Vegas' Wynn Resort.

In short, Villatte has all the experience in the world and has created an authentic French bakery in the heart of Falmouth."

Cookies au Chocolate

18 Cookies

Ingredients

18 tbsp butter

1 cup granulated sugar

2 tsp baking soda

3 large eggs

9 oz milk chocolate, in pieces

9 oz dark chocolate, in pieces

1 cup light brown sugar

4⅓ cups AP flour

½ tbsp salt

Directions

Preheat oven to 315 F.

In a mixer with the paddle attachment, cream the butter and sugars.

Gradually add eggs, scrapping down the bowl as necessary.

Sift together all dry ingredients and add to mixer. Mix until streaky.

Add all chocolate pieces and mix until just combined.

Form dough into 3½ oz pieces and roll into balls.

Place on baking sheet and bake for 14 minutes, turning halfway through the baking.

Falmouth Senior Center

FALMOUTH SENIOR CENTER · CHAPPY CAFÉ
780 Main Street
Falmouth, MA 02540

Chef: Scott Williamson

"Tommy Leonard came into our lives when he arrived in Falmouth, joining my wife Margie as a bartender at the Quarterdeck Restaurant. The bond that was created with us was the beginning of the typical Tommy Leonard relationship, one that he had with the whole world!

We had many dinners with Tommy, and he was a fussy, light eater. But he always had room for a sweet dessert. Tommy was not bashful with Ice Cream Lasagna, his comment was 'Holy Cow'!"

Cook's Note:
If you wish, you can vary the layers using flaked coconut, peanut butter morsels, nuts, etc.

Let your imagination run wild with this FUN to make, FUN to eat dessert!

This recipe is ideal for those summer cookouts.

Ice Cream Lasagna

12+ Servings

Ingredients

3 20-oz jars fudge sauce

3 containers Cool Whip topping

1 to 2 jars Maraschino cherries

3 20-oz jars butterscotch sauce

3 bags Heath Bar Crunch candy

24 ice cream sandwiches

Directions

Lightly Spray bottom and sides of a 9 x 13" pan with vegetable cooking spray.

Place fudge and butterscotch sauce jars in hot water bath to warm (or microwave carefully).

Coat bottom of pan evenly with fudge sauce using a spatula. Unwrap, and place ice cream sandwiches in single layer to fill pan.

Next, evenly cover ice cream sandwiches with butterscotch sauce using spatula. Lightly cover butterscotch layer with Heath Bar Crunch (reserve some to sprinkle on top of last layer of Cool Whip).

Spread a layer of Cool Whip over the entire pan; place another layer of ice cream sandwiches on top of Cool Whip and press down lightly to set.

Cover the top layer of pan completely with fudge sauce. If desired, drizzle butterscotch sauce in a crisscross pattern. Totally cover sauces with Cool Whip.

Sprinkle Cool Whip with remaining Heath Bar Crunch.

Remove stems from cherries and pat dry, evenly place in decorative manner on top of Cool Whip.

Place Ice Cream Lasagna in freezer for 1 to 2 hours. To serve, remove from freezer and cut into desired portion size using a pie knife to plate.

The Village Grocery

& General Store

WOODS HOLE MARKET & PROVISIONS

87 Water Street
Woods Hole, MA 02543
508.540.4792

Owners: Colleen and Branch Parrish
Chef: Barbara Parrish

"The Icing on The Cake"

We all knew and loved Tommy for his incredible stories, charm, curiosity, generosity, and the way he touched so many hearts along his journey.

He loved Mom's Chocolate Birthday Cake. She made it from scratch for family birthdays and Tommy was a lucky recipient.

In true Tommy fashion, he made a point to tell her, "It was the best Chocolate Cake he had ever had! "

Mom's Chocolate Birthday Cake

12 to 16 Servings

Ingredients

Cake

1¾ cup AP flour

¾ cup cocoa powder

1 tsp salt

1 cup milk

1 cup brewed instant coffee

2 cups sugar

2 tsp baking soda

2 eggs

½ cup vegetable oil

1 tsp vanilla extract

Frosting

½ cup butter, melted

3 cups confectioners sugar

1 tsp vanilla extract

⅔ cup Hershey cocoa

⅓ cup milk

1 tbsp brewed instant coffee

Directions

Cake

Preheat oven to 350 F. Butter the sides and bottoms, then lightly flour, two 8-inch round cake pans.

Mix all dry ingredients together. In separate bowl, combine all liquid ingredients, then mix the two together, mixing dry ingredients into liquid.

Pour into pans in equal portions and bake for approximately 30 to 35 minutes or until toothpick comes out clean.

Cool for ½ hour before frosting.

Frosting

Add cocoa to melted butter in medium size mixing bowl and stir.

Add milk and sugar a little at a time and continue to mix.

Beat until smooth.

Add vanilla extract and fold in.

Frosting the Cake

Loosen the cakes by gently running a knife around edge of the pans.

Gently flip the cakes over and put one cake on a plate.

Frost the top of this cake, then add the other layer.

Frost the top gently and spread the frosting evenly around the sides of both layers.

BEAR IN BOOTS BURGER BAR
285 Main Street
Falmouth, MA 02540

Owner / Chef: Kate Ricard

Unfortunately, Kate decided to close Bear in Boots Burger Bar. She did make sure we had one of her children's favorite afternoon snack recipes for the cookbook!!

Cook's Note:
AP flour is unbleached flour.

Power Cookie Recipe

36 Cookies

Ingredients

10 tbsp salted butter, softened

6 tbsp sugar

1 egg

¾ cup AP flour

6 tbsp wheat germ

1 cup oatmeal

½ cup plus 2 tbsp sliced almonds

½ cup dried cranberries

¾ cup brown sugar

1 tsp vanilla extract

1¼ cup whole wheat flour

1⅛ tsp baking soda

6 tbsp oat bran

½ cup plus 2 tbsp Grape Nuts Cereal

½ cup raisins

6 tbsp flax seed

Directions

Preheat oven to 350 F.

Combine flours and baking soda in a bowl and whisk together.

Mix butter and sugars with a paddle attachment until light and airy.

Add vanilla extract; then continuing to mix, add egg.

Add flour mixture and continue mixing until just combined.

Add the remaining ingredients to the batter and mix until just combined.

Scoop 1 heaping tbsp of batter onto a greased baking sheet lined with foil or parchment paper.

Bake for 12 minutes.

THE CASUAL GORMET AND THE CASUAL GOURMET EXPRESS

100 Ter Heun Drive
Falmouth, MA 02540
508.775.4946

Owner / Chef: Olive Chase

Olive Chase founded the Casual Gourmet in 1986.

Rocky Road fudge bars were one of our original, and best-selling pastries. Today, 35 years later, Rocky Road remain a mainstay at every café!

Rocky Road Fudge Bars — 12 Squares

Ingredients

Base

½ cup butter

¼ cup unsweetened chocolate, chopped

1 cup AP flour

2 eggs

1 cup sugar

1 tsp vanilla

1 tsp baking powder

¾ cup chopped nuts

Filling

6 oz cream cheese, softened

2 tbsp AP flour

½ tsp vanilla

¼ cup chopped nuts

2 cups miniature marshmallows

¼ cup butter, softened

½ cup sugar

1 egg

1 cup semisweet chocolate chips

Frosting

¼ cup butter

¼ cup unsweetened chocolate, chopped

3 cups powdered sugar

¼ cup milk

2 oz cream cheese, softened

1 tsp vanilla

Directions

Preheat oven to 350 F. Grease and flour 13 x 9-inch pan.

In large saucepan, melt ½ cup butter and ¼ cup unsweetened chocolate over low heat, stirring until smooth. Remove from heat.

Stir in 1 cup flour and all remaining base ingredients into pot; mix well. Spread in greased and floured pan.

Combine 6 oz. of cream cheese, ¼ cup butter, ½ cup sugar, 2 tbsp flour, ½ tsp vanilla and 1 egg; beat 1 minute at medium speed until smooth and fluffy. Stir in 1/4 cup nuts. Spread over chocolate mixture; sprinkle evenly with chocolate chips.

Bake for 25 to 35 minutes or until toothpick inserted in center comes out clean. Remove from oven; immediately sprinkle with marshmallows. Return to oven; bake an additional 2 minutes.

While marshmallows are baking, in large saucepan, combine ¼ cup butter, milk, 1 oz unsweetened chocolate and 2 oz cream cheese. Cook over low heat, stirring until well blended. Remove from heat; stir in powdered sugar and 1 tsp vanilla until smooth. Immediately pour frosting over puffed marshmallows and lightly swirl with knife to marble. Refrigerate 1 hour or until firm.

Cool on a rack before cutting into bars. Store in refrigerator.

OSTERIA LA CIVETTA

133 Main Street
Falmouth, MA 02540
508.540.1616

Owner: Sara Toselli
Chef: Federico Mainardi

Cook's Note:
To make simple syrup, dissolve ½ cup sugar in ½ cup hot water; let cool to warm before using.

Mascarpone is an Italian cream cheese, available in specialty cheese section of most supermarkets.

Gelatin sheets are a European product—you can substitute 1 tbsp gelatin powder for the sheets.

Tiramisù

10 to 12 Servings

Ingredients

24 oz mascarpone

4 oz sugar

1 cup egg yolks (12 yolks from extra-large eggs)

ladyfingers

simple syrup

24 oz heavy cream

3 gelatin sheets

cold coffee

cocoa powder

Directions

Whip egg yolks and sugar, preferably with a stand mixer, until pale yellow and all sugar is incorporated. Set aside.

Dissolve gelatin sheets in warm simple syrup then whip it with heavy cream. Stop before it's completely whipped.

Incorporate mascarpone into the whipped egg yolks at maximum speed for 10 seconds.

With the help of a spatula, fold whipped cream into the mascarpone and egg yolk mixture.

Let this rest in the fridge for 1 to 2 hours.

When ready to assemble, brush ladyfingers with coffee using a pastry brush. Be careful not to completely drench the ladyfingers so they don't fall apart.

In a pan, layer the mascarpone cream with the ladyfingers.

Sift cocoa powder over the top.

MARTHA'S
281 Main Street
Falmouth, MA 02540

Owner / Chef: Martha Dupree Olney

"Unfortunately, Marthas decided to close her restaurant. However, she did give us a great vegan recipe for the cookbook!"

Vegan Pumpkin Muffins

8 Giant Muffins

Ingredients

½ can organic canned pumpkin

⅓ cup avocado oil

2 tsp apple cider vinegar

2¼ cups AP unbleached flour

1 tbsp pumpkin pie spice

1 cup almond milk

1 cup sugar

1 tbsp real vanilla

1 tbsp sea salt

¾ cup chopped nuts (optional)

Directions

Preheat oven to 375 F. Spray paper muffin cups with non-stick spray.

Whisk together pumpkin, almond milk, avocado oil, sugar, vinegar, and vanilla in a medium bowl.

Whisk together dry ingredients in a separate bowl. Gently combine ingredients and add nuts (if using).

Fill muffin cups ¾ full. Bake for approximately 20 minutes until a toothpick inserted in the center comes out clean.

MEASUREMENTS

CREDITS

Concept
Esther Ann Price

Recipe Compilation
Esther Ann Price
Russ Pelletier

Cover Illustration
Karen Rinaldo

Recipe Editing
Gail Blakely

Design & Printing
New Wave Printing & Design, Inc.
Falmouth, MA

ABOUT THE ART AND ARTIST
Karen Rinaldo

On the cover of the cookbook is a pen and ink drawing by Karen Rinaldo of the front of Tommy's Place located on Elm Arch Way. As she is a visual historian, Karen's illustration depicts the original lines of the 1800's structure of the former Elm Arch Inn.

Her conception of the building was based on the new renovation and the sense of historic eloquence that the property now speaks to, with a new mission and purpose.

THE STORY BEHIND THE TOMMY PORTRAIT

The painting of Tommy Leonard (appearing on page 74) has a permanent home at the far end of the bar at Tommy's favorite meeting place, The Quarterdeck Restaurant. It was Karen's brainchild as what to present Tommy with, in addition to the customary plaque, at the dinner celebrating the Falmouth Historical Society selecting him as the 2013 Heritage Award winner.

Karen described a picture she had seen of Tommy to Mark Schmidt (Executive Director of Museums on the Green), and he informed her they were using that picture for the Awards Program. Karen felt the picture, of Tommy wearing a Falmouth Walk ball cap and sweatshirt, was the perfect depiction of the personality and charisma of the man.

At times Karen struggled with the painting. She wanted to portray Tommy's personality, reflecting an innocent and loving spirit. A man finally content with experiences that life had tossed his way, allowing him to live it out his way.

The picture was supposed to be given to Tommy anonymously, but that only lasted one night. The next day the Falmouth Enterprise had Karen and Tommy meet at the Quarterdeck for pictures of them with the painting. For Karen, it was a thrill to have captured the very essence of the public, yet so private man, and an honor to get his stamp of approval with the twinkle in his eye.

HISTORY OF THE ELM ARCH INN

The History of the Elm Arch Inn is actually the story of three buildings along Main St. in Falmouth. The Silas Jones House, the Conant House, and the Dr. Alexander T. Walker House.

The Silas Jones House, now the Elm Arch Inn, is an important part of Falmouth's cultural heritage. It bears a British cannon ball scar from the war of 1812, a reminder of the exceptional courage Falmouth people demonstrated during that time of hardship.

The Inn began as the home of the town's most prominent whaling family. Upon his death, Capt. Silas Jones left the house to his daughter, Mrs. Harriet Jones Burrill. On January 28, 1814, the British Brig Nimrod opened fire on Falmouth at noon. Miss Ann Freeman refused to leave the house with her mistress. She was boiling meat and remarked that there would be a good many men in town to feed when the day was over. But Miss Freeman left the meat boiling when one of the cannonballs entered the house. Three cannon balls entered the house altogether.

In 1898, Annie Fraser Davis of New Bedford opened the Elm Arch Inn on Palmer Avenue in the Conant house (which is today owned by the Falmouth Historical Society). Not long afterwards, she moved the Inn to the Dr. Alexander T. Walker house (located to the east of the First Congregational Church) remaining there until 1911, when she returned to New Bedford.

On September 30, 1911, Gideon L. Hodgkins bought the Harriet Jones Burrill home on Main Street. Hodgkins remodeled the home, putting on an addition to operate the new Elm Arch Inn.

By 1926, the Elm Arch Inn was moved from Main Street to land immediately south (Elm Arch Way). At this time, it was owned by Ann B. Richardson, the first of three generations to operate the Inn. Her son, Harry, and his wife Flossie became active in the business in 1947. Ann's grandson Pete and his wife Pamela ran the Inn until 2010.

In the beginning the Inn served three meals a day to summer guests and they opened the town's first swimming pool. The Inn was Falmouth's oldest continuous lodging facility, having been in operation for almost 100.

A huge "thank you" to Pete and Pamela Richardson for believing in Tim O'Connell's vision and seeing their family's Elm Arch Inn turned into "Tommy's Place," a vacation home for kids with cancer.

As Miss Ann Freeman said to Mrs. Harriet Jones Burrill, "there will be a great many men (and women and children) in town to feed….."

So, enjoy Tommy's Place Cookbook.

Russ Pelletier

Ellis, James., A Ruinozs and Unhappy War, New England and War of 1812, 2N9, 161
Deyo, Simeon, History of Barnstable County, Part n 1890, 695 and Brown, VÄ of Falmouth, Massachusetts 1976, 78-79 and Starbuck, W'T'* fishery, 1877, 454-512, 536
Starbuck, History of the American Whale Fishery, 129-131.
Wayman, Dorothy, Suckanessett, A History of Falmouth, 1930, Chap. XII
Dyer, Arnold, Hotels and Inns of Falmouth, 1993. 14, VÄ of Falmouth, Massachusetts 1976, 78-79, and Starbuck, WT'* fishery, 1877, 454, 512, 536
History of the Elm Arch Inn